# The Essential Krav Maga

# The Essential Krav Maga

## Christophe Philippe

BLUE SNAKE BOOKS

Berkeley, California

Copyright © 2006 by Chiron Éditeur. All rights reserved. No portion of this book, except for brief review, may be reproduced, stored in a retrieval system, or transmitted in any form or by any means—electronic, mechanical, photocopying, recording, or otherwise—without written permission of the publisher. For information contact Blue Snake Books/Frog, Ltd. c/o North Atlantic Books.

Published by Blue Snake Books/Frog, Ltd.

Blue Snake Books/Frog, Ltd. books are distributed by
North Atlantic Books
P.O. Box 12327
Berkeley, California 94712

Photos: © DR
Cover and book design by Brad Greene

Printed in the United States of America

Blue Snake Books' publications are available through most bookstores. For further information, call 800-337-2665 or visit our websites at www.northatlanticbooks.com or www.bluesnakebooks.com.

Substantial discounts on bulk quantities are available to corporations, professional associations, and other organizations. For details and discount information, contact our special sales department.

PLEASE NOTE: The creators and publishers of this book are not and will not be responsible, in any way whatsoever, for any improper use made by anyone of the information contained in this book. All use of the aforementioned information must be made in accordance with what is permitted by law, and any damage liable to be caused as a result thereof will be the exclusive responsibility of the user. In addition, he or she must adhere strictly to the safety rules contained in the book, both in training and in actual implementation of the information presented herein. This book is intended for use in conjunction with ongoing lessons and personal training with an authorized expert. It is not a substitute for formal training. It is the sole responsibility of every person planning to train in the techniques described in this book to consult a licensed physician in order to obtain complete medical information on his or her personal ability and limitations. The instructions and advice printed in this book are not in any way intended as a substitute for medical, mental, or emotional counseling with a licensed physician or healthcare provider.

This book was originally published by Chiron Éditeur, 25 Rue Monge, 75005 Paris, in 2005, under the title Le Krav-Maga: Techniques et Enchaînements Spécial forces de l'ordre in the Sciences du Combat series. Original ISBN 2-7027-1096-4

Translated from the French by Naomi Blanchard

Library of Congress Cataloging-in-Publication Data

Philippe, Christophe.
    [Krav-Maga, techniques et enchaînements spécial forces de l'ordre. English]
    The essential Krav maga / by Christophe Philippe.
        p. cm.
    Summary: "In this book, the author explains and demonstrates the swift and powerful self-defense and fighting skills of this martial art originally developed for the Israel Defense Forces by Imi Sde-Or (Lichtenfeld)"—Provided by publisher.
    ISBN-13: 978-1-58394-168-3 (trade paper)
    ISBN-10: 1-58394-168-1 (trade paper)
    1. Krav maga.  2. Self-defense.  I. Title.
GV1111.P48 2006
796.8—dc22

2006028867
CIP

2 3 4 5 6 7 8 9 UNITED 12 11 10 09 08 07

# TABLE OF CONTENTS

## Self-Defense Against Long Guns

## Self-Defense Against a Stick Attack, High to Low . . . . . 67

## Self-Defense Against Two Armed Assailants . . . . . 73

## Self-Defense Against Several Unarmed Assailants . . . . . 79

### BRIEF BIOGRAPHY

# ACKNOWLEDGMENTS

I would like to thank Christophe Fossat, Patrick Varela, and David Generaux for their participation in the photo shoots for this book.

I would like to take this opportunity to pay tribute to all of my police and military police colleagues who continually serve and protect our fellow citizens throughout their career.

# PREFACE

In an ever more violent society, self-defense techniques proliferate. Among these, Krav Maga, the Israeli self-defense system perfected in the 1950s by Imi Lichtenfeld, former Chief Instructor of Tashal (the Israeli army), has met with ever-increasing success.

Krav Maga is not just another martial art system based on conventional techniques. It is a modern system characterized by a sound and logical way of thinking that yields natural, practical, and easy techniques based on movements that are simple for the human body.

Originally created for the military and security forces, Krav Maga was adapted for civilians as early as the 1970s. Today, this martial art is taught in many countries and has a very large audience. This is a martial art for everyone, whether you are a man or a woman, or involved with combat sports or not.

Because Krav Maga covers a very broad set of techniques, all types of defenses are studied. Whether one is faced with a single or several assailants, armed or not, Krav Maga covers all possible parries to safeguard one's physical integrity in case of an attack.

This book is not an exhaustive list of all Krav Maga techniques. Its objective is to introduce certain aspects of this pragmatic self-defense system. Different crisis scenarios were selected in order to address the needs of a large number of readers.

No matter which method of self-defense is chosen, only determination and combativeness make it effective. It is important to master simple movements in order to be able to use them optimally to get out of dangerous situations. These movements are why Krav Maga is unique as a self-defense system, emphasizing logic and simplicity in its teachings.

If only a fraction of the techniques in this book allow one person to get home safe and sound, then my goal will have been achieved.

—Christophe Philippe

# Self-Defense Against Bare-Hand Attacks

# Self-Defense Against Punches

## Left-Handed Counter Punch in Defensive Stance

**1.** Use your right palm to defend against a left-hand punch (figure 1).

**2.** At the same time, counter with a left-hand punch (figure 2).

# Right-Handed Counter Punch in Defensive Stance

**3.** Use your left palm to defend against a right-hand punch (figure 3).

**4.** At the same time, counter with a right-hand punch (figure 4).

# Example of Potential Combination Technique Against a Right Punch

**1.** Begin in the defensive position (figure 1).

**2.** Use your left palm to defend against a right punch. At the same time, counter with a right punch (figure 2).

**3.** Hit the groin with an open-handed strike using your right hand (figure 3).

**4.** Deliver a regular kick to the groin using your the right leg (figure 4).

**5.** Continue with a right punch to the face (figure 5).

**6.** Finish by applying leverage to the wrist (figure 6).

# Self-Defense Against Kicks
## Defense Against High Right Kicks
(Simultaneous Kick to the Groin)

**1.** Begin in the defensive position (figure 1).

**2.** Use your left forearm to block while delivering a regular kick to the groin with your left leg (figure 2).

# Defense Against High Left Kicks
## (Two-Forearm Block)

**1.** Begin in the defensive position (figure 1).

**2.** Use the inside of your forearms to block. Begin to block as soon as the assailant begins to kick (figure 2).

**3.** Deliver a left-hand punch to the face (figure 3).

**4.** Follow with a right-hand punch to the face (figure 4)

# Self-Defense Against Choking Attacks

## Defense Against a Left-Side Chokehold

**1.** Begin in the neutral position; the assailant approaches from behind (figure 1).

**2.** Move your right leg out front in order to avoid getting thrown to the ground. At the same time hit the assailant's groin with an open-hand strike and poke your fingers in his eyes (figure 2).

**3, 4.** Bring the assailant to the ground while holding up his arm, and follow with a right-hand punch to the face (figures 3 and 4).

## Defense Against a Left-Side Choking Attack

**1.** Begin in the neutral position; the assailant approaches from behind (figure 1).

**2.** The assailant grabs hold of your neck and applies pressure to your cervical vertebrae (figure 2).

**3.** Use your left leg to block by positioning it behind the assailant (figure 3).

**4.** Throw the assailant to the floor and at the same time hit the groin with an open-hand strike with your left hand (figure 4).

**5.** Climb onto the assailant while holding up his right arm. Deliver a right-hand punch to the face (figure 5).

# Self-Defense Against Knife Attacks

## Defense Against a Frontal Threat I

(Direct Grab of Knife-Wielding Hand technique)

**1.** Begin in the neutral position, facing the threat at arm's length (figure 1).

**2.** Grab the knife-wielding hand (figure 2).

**3.** Follow with a right-hand punch to the face while holding the knife-wielding arm (figure 3).

**4.** Apply leverage to the assailant's wrist with both hands (figure 4).

**5.** Bring the assailant to the floor by applying pressure to the palm of his hand (figure 5).

**6.** Slam the assailant's elbow on the ground (figure 6).

**7, 8.** Take the knife by "scraping" it from his hand and pressing your fingers into the palm of his hand (figures 7 and 8).

# Defense Against a Frontal Threat II

(Deflection of the Arm towards the Outside
technique)

**1.** Begin in the
neutral position
facing the threat
at arm's length
(figure 1).

**2.** Deflect the
knife-wielding
hand with the
palm of your
right hand
(figure 2).

**3, 4.** Hold the knife-wielding hand and deliver a regular kick to the groin (figures 3 and 4).

**5.** Deliver a
right-hand punch
to the face
(figure 5).

**6.** Begin to
apply leverage to
the assailant's
wrist (figure 6).

**7, 8.** Grab the knife from his hand (figures 7 and 8).

# Close-Up on Disarming the Assailant, applicable to the two techniques

**1.** Grab the knife-wielding hand (figure 1).

**2.** Twist the wrist with your other hand (figure 2).

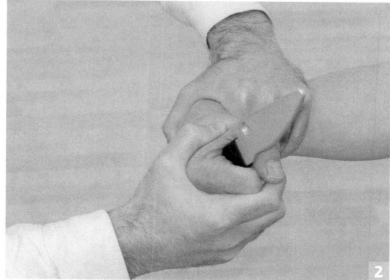

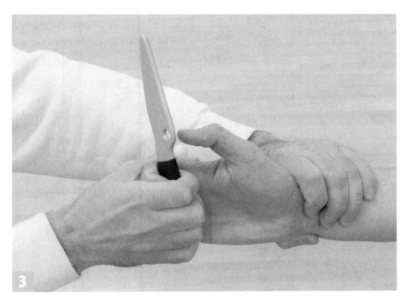

**3.** Forcefully dig your fingers into the palm of his hand (figure 3).

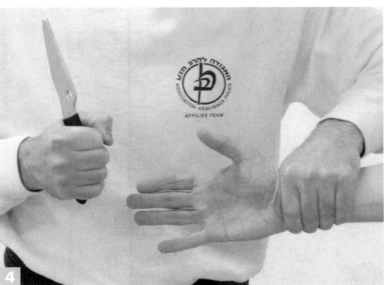

**4.** With a sharp movement, rip the knife from the assailant's hand so that you can grab the knife's handle (figure 4).

# Defense Against a Knife Attack, High to Low at a Short Distance

## Blocking Against

**1.** Begin in the neutral position (figure 1).

**2.** The assailant is in front of you, and he attacks suddenly. Use the forearm defense (right) and prepare for a counterattack. Punch the assailant in the chin while grabbing the knife-wielding hand with a sweeping motion. Neutralize the knife-wielding hand by keeping hold of it while exerting forward pressure (figure 2).

**3.** Deliver a knee to the groin (figure 3).

**4.** Hit the assailant's neck with your fist (figure 4).

**5.** As soon as the assailant begins to weaken, bring his arm forward (figure 5).

**6, 7.** Grab hold of the assailant's wrist by sinking your fingers into the knife-wielding hand (figures 6 and 7).

**8.** Use a "scraping" motion to remove the knife from the assailant's hand. Move a safe distance away.

## Simple Counterattack

Note: From this distance, if the timing is right, it is possible to simply counter the attack with a punch. Your punch will hit the assailant before the knife hits you, and the assailant will step back from the impact.

**1.** Begin in the undefended position (figure 1).

**2.** Deliver a right-hand punch to the face.

# Self-Defense Against Guns

# Self-Defense Against Handguns

## Defense Against a Threat to the Head

**1.** Begin in neutral stance facing the threat to the head at arm's length (figure 1).

**2.** Thrust your hand upward while ducking (figure 2).

**3.** You are now able to grab the gun and to get out of the line of fire. Take one step forward while lowering and holding the gun-wielding hand. Follow with a right-hand punch to the chin (figure 3).

**4.** Use your body weight to apply
heavy pressure on the gun while pushing towards the assailant's body. The
elbow of the gun-wielding arm should
remain nearly straight, causing the
gun to point down and to the side.

Grab the back of the gun: this is done
by grabbing the gun from behind
and not going across the line of fire
(figure 4).

**5.** Twist the gun in the assailant's hand, perpendicular to its initial position, in such a way that 1) the assailant no longer has a tight hold on the gun; and 2) his trigger finger is useless while the gun is being taken away (figure 5).

**6.** Grab the gun with a sharp and horizontal movement, step back, and retreat to a secure place (figure 6).

# Defense Against a Gun Threat with Distance

**1.** Begin in neutral position facing a mid-section threat, at arm's length (figure 1).

**2.** The assailant is going to push you (figure 2).

**3.** Use the assailant's momentum to move your body away from the gun's axis. At the same time, grab the barrel and the breech (figure 3).

**4.** Leap one step forward while lowering and holding the gun-wielding hand, and simultaneously throw a right-handed punch to the chin (figure 4).

**5, 6.** Twist the gun in the assailant's hand, perpendicular to its initial position, in such a way that 1) the assailant no longer has a tight hold on the gun; and 2) his trigger finger is useless while the gun is being taken away (figures 5 and 6).

**7.** Grab the gun with a sharp and horizontal movement, step back, and retreat to a secure place (figure 7).

## Close-Up Look at Disarming the Assailant

**1.** Grab the gun with your thumb pointing down. Your right hand strengthens the hold from the back of the gun (figure 1).

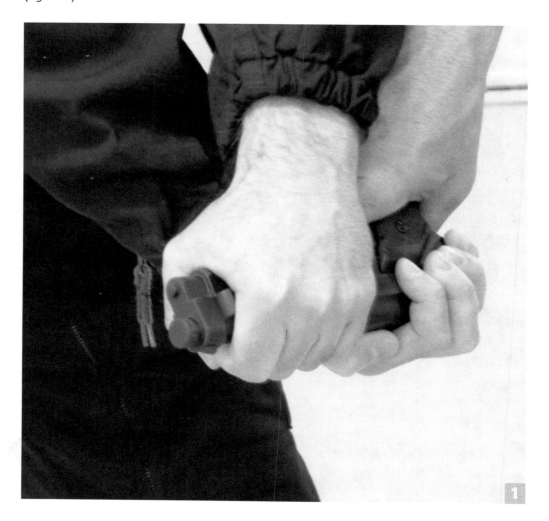

**2.** Twist the gun perpendicular to its initial position. Take the gun away with a quick movement (figure 2).

# Protecting Others Against a Handgun Threat

## Standing to the Left of the Companion or VIP (Arm Push)

**1.** You are standing to the left and very close to your companion (figure 1).

**2.** The assailant threatens with a gun, relatively close to you and your companion (figure 2).

**3.** As you push your companion out of the way, leap forward (figure 3).

**4.** Push the assailant's gun-wielding hand down as you grab the weapon (barrel and breech) away from him (figure 4).

**5.** At the same time, throw a right-hand punch to the assailant's chin. Exert strong pressure on the gun using your body weight, all the while pushing towards the assailant's body. The elbow of the gun-wielding hand remains almost straight, causing the gun to point down and to the side (figure 5).

**6.** Grab the back of the gun. This is done by grabbing the gun from behind and not going across the line of fire (figure 6).

**7.** Twist the gun in the assailant's hand, perpendicular to its initial position, in such a way that 1) the assailant no longer has a tight hold on the gun; and 2) his trigger finger is useless while the gun is being taken away (figure 7).

**8.** Grab the gun with a sharp and horizontal movement, step back, and retreat to a secure place (figure 8).

# Standing to the Left of Your Companion (Shoulder Pull)

**1.** You are standing to the left and slightly behind your companion's shoulder; the distance between you and your companion may be slightly greater than in the previous technique (figure 1).

**2.** The assailant threatens with the gun. The distance between you and the assailant is relatively close (figure 2).

**3.** Grab your companion's shoulder and pull backwards, propelling yourself forward to grab the assailant's gun (figure 3).

**4.** At the same time, follow with a right-hand punch to the chin (figure 4).

**5.** Exert strong pressure using your body weight on the gun while pushing towards the assailant's body. The elbow of the gun-wielding hand remains almost straight, causing the gun to point down and to the side (figure 5).

**6.** Grab the back of the gun. This is done by grabbing from behind and not going across the gun's line of fire. Twist the gun in the assailant's hand, perpendicular to its initial position, in such a way that 1) the assailant no longer has a tight hold on the gun; and 2) his trigger finger is useless while the gun is being taken away (figure 6).

**7.** Grab the gun with a sharp and horizontal movement, step back, and retreat to a secure place (figure 7).

## Close-Up Look at the Two Positions

**1.** Use the forearm to push your companion out of the way (figure 1).

**2.** Use your hand to pull your companion's shoulder backwards (figure 2).

## Approaching an Armed Assailant from Behind Who is Threatening a Third Party

**1.** An assailant is threatening someone from the front with a handgun (short distance) (figure 1).

**2.** Approach the assailant from behind. Put your left leg forward, making sure to not enter into the assailant's field of vision (figure 2).

**3.** Throw yourself forward in order to grab the gun. Lead with your hands rather than your body in order to surprise the assailant. Grab the wrist and the gun (barrel and breech) (figure 3).

**4.** Turn the gun on the assailant by applying pressure on the wrist and hand (figure 4).

**5.** Disarm the assailant by pulling the gun towards you and simultaneously hitting the assailant in the chest with the gun's barrel (figure 5).

Grab the gun with a sharp and horizontal movement, step back, and retreat to a secure place.

# Taking the Gun Away
# from the Assailant

**1.** Grab the assailant's wrist and the barrel/ breech of the gun (figure 1).

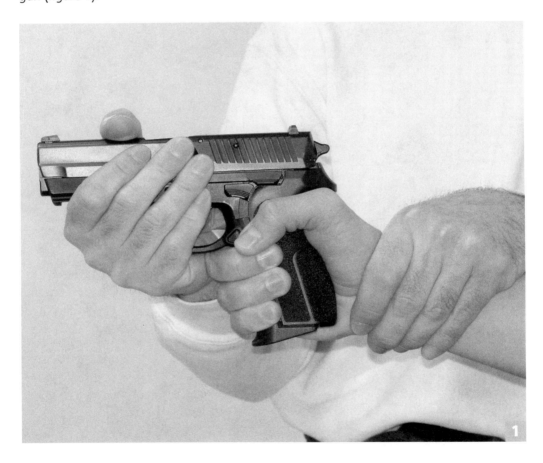

# Self-Defense Against Long-barreled Gun

## Frontal Threat

(Sequence of moves starting on the left side)

**1.** Begin in the neutral position facing a threat with a long gun pointed at your head (figure 1).

**2.** Push the barrel of the gun aside using your left arm, and simultaneously move out of the line of fire (figure 2).

**3.** Take a small step forward and place your forearms against the gun in order to exert some control over it (figure 3).

**4.** Grab the gun and slightly lift it up, making way for a normal kick to the groin with your left leg. In the event the gun is a submachine gun, make sure to lift the gun sufficiently to avoid hitting the magazine (figure 4).

**5.** Take a step forward with your right leg in order to hit the assailant's head with the barrel of the gun (figure 5).

**6.** Take the gun away from the assailant with a straight quick movement while moving a safe distance from him, and then retreat to a secure place (figure 6).

## Frontal Threat

(Sequence of moves starting
on the right side)

**1.** Begin in the
neutral position
facing a threat
with a long gun
aimed at your
head (figure 1).

**2.** Use your right arm to move the barrel of the gun to the side while simultaneously moving yourself out of the line of fire (figure 2).

**3.** Take one small step forward, and grab the gun with your left hand (figure 3).

**4.** Follow with a normal kick to the groin with the left leg (figure 4).

**5.** While continuing to hold on to the gun with the left hand, follow with a right-hand punch to the chin (figure 5).

**6.** Place your right hand on the gun, going under the assailant's left arm (figure 6).

**7.** Disarm the assailant by applying pressure to the joint of his left arm: this move is accomplished by moving the right leg forward (figure 7).

**8.** Grab the gun away from the assailant, hit him on the head with the butt of the gun, and move a safe distance away (figures 8 and 9).

# Self-Defense Against a Stick Attack, High to Low

# Self-Defense Against a Stick Attack, High to Low

**1.** Stand out of range of the stick (figure 1).

**2.** Just as the assailant begins to strike, extend your left arm so that it slides against the assailant's stick-wielding forearm or, at worst, against the stick itself. Your head goes forward, followed by your body. Simultaneously, finish the move with a right-hand punch to hit the assailant's face (figure 2).

**3–5.** Deliver a knee then a regular kick to the groin, followed by a right-hand punch to the face (figures 3, 4, 5).

5

**6.** Move your right foot back, while you continue to hold (figure 6).

**7.** Shift your entire body weight to the right as you dis-arm the assailant with a sharp chest movement (figure 7).

# Self-Defense Against Two Armed Assailants

# Self-Defense Against
# Two Armed Assailants

**1.** You are facing two assailants, one armed with a knife, the other with a stick (figure 1).

**2.** Block against the first attacker, who is wielding a knife (figure 2).

**3.** Turn the first assailant to the side in order to be in a good position to attack the second assailant (figure 3).

**4.** Block against the second attacker, who is wielding a stick (figure 4).

**5, 6, 7.** Turn the second assailant so that he shields you from the first assailant. Push the second assailant onto the first and make a run for it (figures 5, 6, 7).

When faced with two assailants, it is always a good rule of thumb to be on the outside so as to avoid turning your back to an assailant.

# Self-Defense Against
# Several Unarmed Assailants

## Defense Against Three Assailants (held by two)

**1.** Two assailants hold you by the wrists and you face a third assailant (figure 1).

**2.** Deliver a regular kick with your left leg to the first assailant as he approaches (figure 2).

**3.** Using the same leg, deliver a side kick to the assailant on your left (figure 3).

**4.** Next, kick the assailant to your right in the groin with your right leg (figure 4).

**5, 6.** Free your-self from the original hold by lifting your elbow and pulling the arm downward (figures 5 and 6).

**7, 8.** Turn the assailant on your right around so that he is placed between you and the other two assailants (figures 7 and 8).

# Clearing the Arm

**1.** Briskly thrust the arm downward and the elbow upward.

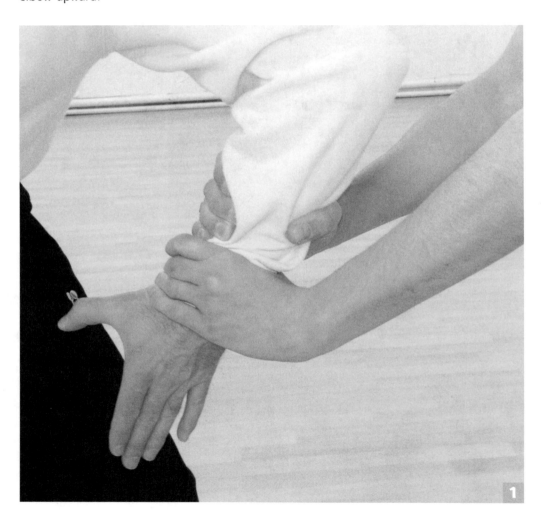

# Defense Against a Crowd (back against a wall)

Note: Make your move early before the assailants get too close.

**1.** You have your back against a wall facing several assailants (figure 1).

**2.** Gather momentum from behind by pushing off the wall (figure 2).

**3.** Leap forward, arms forming a triangle, pulling your head in and clenching your fists (figure 3).

**4, 5.** Your chest is leaning forward (figures 4 and 5).

Extract yourself using the assailants.

# Close-Up Look at the Position

**1.** Your chest is leaning forward and your fists are clenched (figure 1).

**2.** Clench your fists and form a triangle with your forearms (figure 2).

**Imi Lichtenfeld** and **Christophe Philippe** in Netanya, Israel, 1994

# BRIEF BIOGRAPHY

## Imi Lichtenfeld, Founder of Krav Maga

IMI LICHTENFELD was born in 1910 in Bratislava, Czechoslovakia. He was inspired by his father Samuel—a former circus acrobat and wrestler, physical education teacher, Chief Detective, and instructor for the Municipal Police Department, known not only for his self-defense teachings but for his many arrests. Imi also participated in multiple sports, dedicating himself to gymnastics, wrestling, and boxing. Over a ten-year period, he was actively involved in a large number of competitions which he often won (mostly wrestling).

As fascism emerged in the 1930s, Imi surrounded himself with a group of young athletes who made it their mission to protect the local Jewish population by fighting against the fascist militias. He was also involved in numerous brawls that made him reflect upon the differences between street fighting and sport competitions, and as a result of these circumstances, the first principles of Krav Maga were born.

Because of this activity, Imi quickly became unpopular with local authorities and was forced to leave Bratislava. His journey from there to Israel lasted three years. Upon arrival, he joined the Haganah (Jewish paramilitary group) and first taught basic self-defense techniques. He then continued teaching within Tashal, the Israeli army. It was there that, working over the course of twenty years, he perfected his

Krav Maga system while looking after the instructors of the Army's elite units.

Later, Krav Maga—recognized by the Israel Department of Education—became part of civilian life, both in the private and public sectors. It eventually spread throughout the world and is now taught in many countries, including France and the United States.

Krav Maga, as developed by Imi, is built on moral and human values that underscore the importance of integrity, humility, and respect for others.

Imi Lichtenfeld died on January 9, 1998, at the age of 87.

# ABOUT THE AUTHOR

CHRISTOPHE PHILIPPE, a French Police Sergeant in the SPHP (Protection services for important national and foreign dignitaries), discovered Krav Maga in 1994 while taking part in a training program under the tutelage of Richard Douïeb.

After being involved with many martial arts and combat sports, he decided to dedicate himself exclusively to Krav Maga, as he is convinced of its effectiveness and considers it to be completely suitable for law enforcement.

In 1996, Philippe spent time in Israel to complete his training and was introduced by his teacher, Richard Douïeb, to Imi Lichtenfeld, founder of Krav Maga, with whom Philippe shared his plan to introduce this self-defense system to the French Police.

Back in France, with the approval of the European Federation of Krav Maga, he instituted introductory training seminars exclusively for law enforcement personnel.

In 1999, Christophe Philippe created the Association of Krav Maga Police (AKMP). Its objective is to promote and teach Krav Maga within law enforcement in France.

Christophe Philippe continues to teach Krav Maga to police and civilians and to further his own education under the tutelage of Richard Douïeb, the discipline's official representative in Europe.

## ASSOCIATION KRAV MAGA POLICE

202 rue de la roquette
75011 PARIS
FRANCE
http://www.krav-maga.fr
akmp@krav-maga.fr